MW00475043

Colorpedia Notebook

Organize your colors

by Radu Frăsie

ISBN: 9781086295863

Table of Contents

Thank You!

Thanks for buying the Colorpedia Notebook!
I hope you will enjoy using it!

I have a gift for you:

FREE
COLORING PAGES

Visit my website and download all the FREE files
uploaded so far:

www.radufrasie.com

QUALITY ASSURANCE

As a quality assurance for you, I offer full video flip
through from my books on my website. In this
way, you can see the whole content of my books
before buying them.

How to use this Notebook

This notebook will help you organize your colors and keep all of them in one place. It is your best companion while coloring, helping you find the perfect colors for your artworks in a quick and easy way. Following you will find instructions on how to use the different types of charts from this notebook.

1. Color Charts - by set

Organize your colors by set. Because most manufacturers provide coloring supplies in sets of 12 pieces (or multiple - 24, 36, 48 etc.) the color charts contain 48 slots divided in 2 columns of 24 slots, allowing you to use one column or one page for a set of colors or multiple consecutive pages for a larger set.

Fill the „Color" cell with your color and write in the cell beside it the name or the code of the pencil used to create that color (Fig. 1). Repeat this action until you create a chart with all the colors from a set. The next time when you want to use that specific set of pencils you can take a look at this chart, choose the color you want to use in your artwork and find beside it the code of the pencil you need to use to recreate that color.

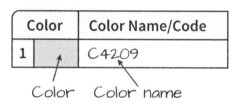

Fig. 1 - Color Charts - by set

2. Color Charts - by color

This type of charts will help you organize your coloring supplies by color. For example, if you have multiple sets of colors and you want to use a blue color in your artwork, you will have a chart with all your blue colors next to each other helping you decide which shade of blue fits better in your artwork. In order to use this type of charts, first you need to have your colors recorded in the color charts by set (the previous charts), because this will help you identify the colors.

The „Color charts - by color" are divided in 9 colors (or group of colors) each of them having a „Color chart" and 2 „Identifier tables". Following you will find an example of how to use them.

Let's say that you create a Color Chart (by set) for your „X Company" colored pencils set on the page 24 of the this notebook and you place the blue color „C4283" on position 1 of the chart (Fig. 2).

Color	Color Name/Code
1	C4283

Fig. 2 - Color Charts - by set

Next, in the Blue Color Chart (by color) you color the „A1" cell with the same blue pencil (Fig. 3). Find the „A1" position in the identifier table of blue colors and write the page and position at which this shade of blue can be found - in our case page 24, position 1 (Fig. 4) (You will fill the other cells A2, A3, A4 .... O15 with other shades of blue as you add them to your collection). Maybe it sounds a little complicated, but just try it, it's much easier than it sounds.

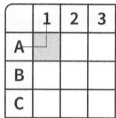

Fig. 3 - Color Charts - by color

#	Pag.	Pos.
A1	24	1

Fig. 4 - Identifier Table

Now, every time when you want to use a blue color, you can take the Blue Color Chart, choose the best shade of blue for your artwork and find in the identifier table the page and position where the information for this shade of blue are stored. For example, if you like the blue color from the position „A1" in the Blue Color Chart (Fig. 3), in the identifier table you will see that „A1" shade of blue is stored at page 24 on position 1 (Fig. 4). If you navigate to the page 24 you will see at position 1 that this shade of blue is a „C4283" color from the „X Company" color set (Fig. 2).

3. Color Blending Charts

In this type of charts you can record your color blendings in order to be able to reproduce them in a future artwork. Create your color blend in the first cell of the table and write beside it the pencil codes you have used to create that particular blend (Fig. 5).

Color Blending	Color Names/Codes
	C4209 + C4478 + 3204

Fig. 5 - Color Blending Charts

4. Color Palettes Charts

You can use this charts to record your favorite color palettes to be able to reproduce them in a future project. The charts are not divided in smaller palettes in order to allow you to create color palettes with any number of colors you like. Just create your color palletes and leave an empty row between them (Fig. 6).

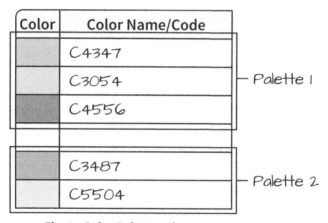

Fig. 6 - Color Palettes Charts

5. Notes

Here you can write any kind of notes you like.

6. Content tables

The content tables from the begining of this notebook are created to help you keep track of your color charts. You can write inside them the name of your charts and the pages at which they can be found.

Table of Contents

Title	Page

Title	Page

Title	Page

Title	Page

Color Charts
by set

Chart Title

Color		Color Name/Code	Color		Color Name/Code
1			25		
2			26		
3			27		
4			28		
5			29		
6			30		
7			31		
8			32		
9			33		
10			34		
11			35		
12			36		
13			37		
14			38		
15			39		
16			40		
17			41		
18			42		
19			43		
20			44		
21			45		
22			46		
23			47		
24			48		

Chart Title

Color	Color Name/Code	Color	Color Name/Code
1		25	
2		26	
3		27	
4		28	
5		29	
6		30	
7		31	
8		32	
9		33	
10		34	
11		35	
12		36	
13		37	
14		38	
15		39	
16		40	
17		41	
18		42	
19		43	
20		44	
21		45	
22		46	
23		47	
24		48	

Chart Title

Color	Color Name/Code	Color	Color Name/Code
1		25	
2		26	
3		27	
4		28	
5		29	
6		30	
7		31	
8		32	
9		33	
10		34	
11		35	
12		36	
13		37	
14		38	
15		39	
16		40	
17		41	
18		42	
19		43	
20		44	
21		45	
22		46	
23		47	
24		48	

Chart Title

Color	Color Name/Code	Color	Color Name/Code
1		25	
2		26	
3		27	
4		28	
5		29	
6		30	
7		31	
8		32	
9		33	
10		34	
11		35	
12		36	
13		37	
14		38	
15		39	
16		40	
17		41	
18		42	
19		43	
20		44	
21		45	
22		46	
23		47	
24		48	

Chart Title

Color	Color Name/Code	Color	Color Name/Code
1		25	
2		26	
3		27	
4		28	
5		29	
6		30	
7		31	
8		32	
9		33	
10		34	
11		35	
12		36	
13		37	
14		38	
15		39	
16		40	
17		41	
18		42	
19		43	
20		44	
21		45	
22		46	
23		47	
24		48	

Chart Title

Color	Color Name/Code	Color	Color Name/Code
1		25	
2		26	
3		27	
4		28	
5		29	
6		30	
7		31	
8		32	
9		33	
10		34	
11		35	
12		36	
13		37	
14		38	
15		39	
16		40	
17		41	
18		42	
19		43	
20		44	
21		45	
22		46	
23		47	
24		48	

Chart Title

Color	Color Name/Code	Color	Color Name/Code
1		25	
2		26	
3		27	
4		28	
5		29	
6		30	
7		31	
8		32	
9		33	
10		34	
11		35	
12		36	
13		37	
14		38	
15		39	
16		40	
17		41	
18		42	
19		43	
20		44	
21		45	
22		46	
23		47	
24		48	

Chart Title

Color	Color Name/Code	Color	Color Name/Code
1		25	
2		26	
3		27	
4		28	
5		29	
6		30	
7		31	
8		32	
9		33	
10		34	
11		35	
12		36	
13		37	
14		38	
15		39	
16		40	
17		41	
18		42	
19		43	
20		44	
21		45	
22		46	
23		47	
24		48	

Chart Title

Color	Color Name/Code	Color	Color Name/Code
1		25	
2		26	
3		27	
4		28	
5		29	
6		30	
7		31	
8		32	
9		33	
10		34	
11		35	
12		36	
13		37	
14		38	
15		39	
16		40	
17		41	
18		42	
19		43	
20		44	
21		45	
22		46	
23		47	
24		48	

Color	Color Name/Code	Color	Color Name/Code
Chart Title			

Color	Color Name/Code	Color	Color Name/Code
1		25	
2		26	
3		27	
4		28	
5		29	
6		30	
7		31	
8		32	
9		33	
10		34	
11		35	
12		36	
13		37	
14		38	
15		39	
16		40	
17		41	
18		42	
19		43	
20		44	
21		45	
22		46	
23		47	
24		48	

Chart Title

Color	Color Name/Code	Color	Color Name/Code
1		25	
2		26	
3		27	
4		28	
5		29	
6		30	
7		31	
8		32	
9		33	
10		34	
11		35	
12		36	
13		37	
14		38	
15		39	
16		40	
17		41	
18		42	
19		43	
20		44	
21		45	
22		46	
23		47	
24		48	

Chart Title			

Color	Color Name/Code	Color	Color Name/Code
1		25	
2		26	
3		27	
4		28	
5		29	
6		30	
7		31	
8		32	
9		33	
10		34	
11		35	
12		36	
13		37	
14		38	
15		39	
16		40	
17		41	
18		42	
19		43	
20		44	
21		45	
22		46	
23		47	
24		48	

Chart Title

Color	Color Name/Code	Color	Color Name/Code
1		25	
2		26	
3		27	
4		28	
5		29	
6		30	
7		31	
8		32	
9		33	
10		34	
11		35	
12		36	
13		37	
14		38	
15		39	
16		40	
17		41	
18		42	
19		43	
20		44	
21		45	
22		46	
23		47	
24		48	

Chart Title

Color	Color Name/Code	Color	Color Name/Code
1		25	
2		26	
3		27	
4		28	
5		29	
6		30	
7		31	
8		32	
9		33	
10		34	
11		35	
12		36	
13		37	
14		38	
15		39	
16		40	
17		41	
18		42	
19		43	
20		44	
21		45	
22		46	
23		47	
24		48	

Chart Title

Color	Color Name/Code	Color	Color Name/Code
1		25	
2		26	
3		27	
4		28	
5		29	
6		30	
7		31	
8		32	
9		33	
10		34	
11		35	
12		36	
13		37	
14		38	
15		39	
16		40	
17		41	
18		42	
19		43	
20		44	
21		45	
22		46	
23		47	
24		48	

Color	Color Name/Code	Color	Color Name/Code
1		25	
2		26	
3		27	
4		28	
5		29	
6		30	
7		31	
8		32	
9		33	
10		34	
11		35	
12		36	
13		37	
14		38	
15		39	
16		40	
17		41	
18		42	
19		43	
20		44	
21		45	
22		46	
23		47	
24		48	

Chart Title

Color	Color Name/Code	Color	Color Name/Code
1		25	
2		26	
3		27	
4		28	
5		29	
6		30	
7		31	
8		32	
9		33	
10		34	
11		35	
12		36	
13		37	
14		38	
15		39	
16		40	
17		41	
18		42	
19		43	
20		44	
21		45	
22		46	
23		47	
24		48	

Chart Title

Color	Color Name/Code	Color	Color Name/Code
1		25	
2		26	
3		27	
4		28	
5		29	
6		30	
7		31	
8		32	
9		33	
10		34	
11		35	
12		36	
13		37	
14		38	
15		39	
16		40	
17		41	
18		42	
19		43	
20		44	
21		45	
22		46	
23		47	
24		48	

Chart Title			

Color	Color Name/Code	Color	Color Name/Code
1		25	
2		26	
3		27	
4		28	
5		29	
6		30	
7		31	
8		32	
9		33	
10		34	
11		35	
12		36	
13		37	
14		38	
15		39	
16		40	
17		41	
18		42	
19		43	
20		44	
21		45	
22		46	
23		47	
24		48	

Chart Title

Color	Color Name/Code	Color	Color Name/Code
1		25	
2		26	
3		27	
4		28	
5		29	
6		30	
7		31	
8		32	
9		33	
10		34	
11		35	
12		36	
13		37	
14		38	
15		39	
16		40	
17		41	
18		42	
19		43	
20		44	
21		45	
22		46	
23		47	
24		48	

Chart Title

Color	Color Name/Code	Color	Color Name/Code
1		25	
2		26	
3		27	
4		28	
5		29	
6		30	
7		31	
8		32	
9		33	
10		34	
11		35	
12		36	
13		37	
14		38	
15		39	
16		40	
17		41	
18		42	
19		43	
20		44	
21		45	
22		46	
23		47	
24		48	

Chart Title

Color	Color Name/Code	Color	Color Name/Code
1		25	
2		26	
3		27	
4		28	
5		29	
6		30	
7		31	
8		32	
9		33	
10		34	
11		35	
12		36	
13		37	
14		38	
15		39	
16		40	
17		41	
18		42	
19		43	
20		44	
21		45	
22		46	
23		47	
24		48	

Chart Title

Color	Color Name/Code	Color	Color Name/Code
1		25	
2		26	
3		27	
4		28	
5		29	
6		30	
7		31	
8		32	
9		33	
10		34	
11		35	
12		36	
13		37	
14		38	
15		39	
16		40	
17		41	
18		42	
19		43	
20		44	
21		45	
22		46	
23		47	
24		48	

Chart Title

Color	Color Name/Code	Color	Color Name/Code
1		25	
2		26	
3		27	
4		28	
5		29	
6		30	
7		31	
8		32	
9		33	
10		34	
11		35	
12		36	
13		37	
14		38	
15		39	
16		40	
17		41	
18		42	
19		43	
20		44	
21		45	
22		46	
23		47	
24		48	

Chart Title

	Color	Color Name/Code		Color	Color Name/Code
1			25		
2			26		
3			27		
4			28		
5			29		
6			30		
7			31		
8			32		
9			33		
10			34		
11			35		
12			36		
13			37		
14			38		
15			39		
16			40		
17			41		
18			42		
19			43		
20			44		
21			45		
22			46		
23			47		
24			48		

Chart Title

Color	Color Name/Code	Color	Color Name/Code
1		25	
2		26	
3		27	
4		28	
5		29	
6		30	
7		31	
8		32	
9		33	
10		34	
11		35	
12		36	
13		37	
14		38	
15		39	
16		40	
17		41	
18		42	
19		43	
20		44	
21		45	
22		46	
23		47	
24		48	

Chart Title

Color	Color Name/Code	Color	Color Name/Code
1		25	
2		26	
3		27	
4		28	
5		29	
6		30	
7		31	
8		32	
9		33	
10		34	
11		35	
12		36	
13		37	
14		38	
15		39	
16		40	
17		41	
18		42	
19		43	
20		44	
21		45	
22		46	
23		47	
24		48	

Chart Title

Color	Color Name/Code	Color	Color Name/Code
1		25	
2		26	
3		27	
4		28	
5		29	
6		30	
7		31	
8		32	
9		33	
10		34	
11		35	
12		36	
13		37	
14		38	
15		39	
16		40	
17		41	
18		42	
19		43	
20		44	
21		45	
22		46	
23		47	
24		48	

Chart Title

Color	Color Name/Code	Color	Color Name/Code
1		25	
2		26	
3		27	
4		28	
5		29	
6		30	
7		31	
8		32	
9		33	
10		34	
11		35	
12		36	
13		37	
14		38	
15		39	
16		40	
17		41	
18		42	
19		43	
20		44	
21		45	
22		46	
23		47	
24		48	

Chart Title

Color	Color Name/Code	Color	Color Name/Code
1		25	
2		26	
3		27	
4		28	
5		29	
6		30	
7		31	
8		32	
9		33	
10		34	
11		35	
12		36	
13		37	
14		38	
15		39	
16		40	
17		41	
18		42	
19		43	
20		44	
21		45	
22		46	
23		47	
24		48	

Chart Title

Color	Color Name/Code	Color	Color Name/Code
1		25	
2		26	
3		27	
4		28	
5		29	
6		30	
7		31	
8		32	
9		33	
10		34	
11		35	
12		36	
13		37	
14		38	
15		39	
16		40	
17		41	
18		42	
19		43	
20		44	
21		45	
22		46	
23		47	
24		48	

Chart Title

Color	Color Name/Code	Color	Color Name/Code
1		25	
2		26	
3		27	
4		28	
5		29	
6		30	
7		31	
8		32	
9		33	
10		34	
11		35	
12		36	
13		37	
14		38	
15		39	
16		40	
17		41	
18		42	
19		43	
20		44	
21		45	
22		46	
23		47	
24		48	

Chart Title

Color	Color Name/Code	Color	Color Name/Code
1		25	
2		26	
3		27	
4		28	
5		29	
6		30	
7		31	
8		32	
9		33	
10		34	
11		35	
12		36	
13		37	
14		38	
15		39	
16		40	
17		41	
18		42	
19		43	
20		44	
21		45	
22		46	
23		47	
24		48	

Chart Title

Color	Color Name/Code	Color	Color Name/Code
1		25	
2		26	
3		27	
4		28	
5		29	
6		30	
7		31	
8		32	
9		33	
10		34	
11		35	
12		36	
13		37	
14		38	
15		39	
16		40	
17		41	
18		42	
19		43	
20		44	
21		45	
22		46	
23		47	
24		48	

Chart Title

Color	Color Name/Code	Color	Color Name/Code
1		25	
2		26	
3		27	
4		28	
5		29	
6		30	
7		31	
8		32	
9		33	
10		34	
11		35	
12		36	
13		37	
14		38	
15		39	
16		40	
17		41	
18		42	
19		43	
20		44	
21		45	
22		46	
23		47	
24		48	

Chart Title

Color	Color Name/Code	Color	Color Name/Code
1		25	
2		26	
3		27	
4		28	
5		29	
6		30	
7		31	
8		32	
9		33	
10		34	
11		35	
12		36	
13		37	
14		38	
15		39	
16		40	
17		41	
18		42	
19		43	
20		44	
21		45	
22		46	
23		47	
24		48	

Chart Title

Color	Color Name/Code	Color	Color Name/Code
1		25	
2		26	
3		27	
4		28	
5		29	
6		30	
7		31	
8		32	
9		33	
10		34	
11		35	
12		36	
13		37	
14		38	
15		39	
16		40	
17		41	
18		42	
19		43	
20		44	
21		45	
22		46	
23		47	
24		48	

Chart Title

Color	Color Name/Code	Color	Color Name/Code
1		25	
2		26	
3		27	
4		28	
5		29	
6		30	
7		31	
8		32	
9		33	
10		34	
11		35	
12		36	
13		37	
14		38	
15		39	
16		40	
17		41	
18		42	
19		43	
20		44	
21		45	
22		46	
23		47	
24		48	

Chart Title

Color	Color Name/Code	Color	Color Name/Code
1		25	
2		26	
3		27	
4		28	
5		29	
6		30	
7		31	
8		32	
9		33	
10		34	
11		35	
12		36	
13		37	
14		38	
15		39	
16		40	
17		41	
18		42	
19		43	
20		44	
21		45	
22		46	
23		47	
24		48	

Chart Title

Color	Color Name/Code	Color	Color Name/Code
1		25	
2		26	
3		27	
4		28	
5		29	
6		30	
7		31	
8		32	
9		33	
10		34	
11		35	
12		36	
13		37	
14		38	
15		39	
16		40	
17		41	
18		42	
19		43	
20		44	
21		45	
22		46	
23		47	
24		48	

| Chart Title | | | |

Color	Color Name/Code	Color	Color Name/Code
1		25	
2		26	
3		27	
4		28	
5		29	
6		30	
7		31	
8		32	
9		33	
10		34	
11		35	
12		36	
13		37	
14		38	
15		39	
16		40	
17		41	
18		42	
19		43	
20		44	
21		45	
22		46	
23		47	
24		48	

Chart Title

Color	Color Name/Code	Color	Color Name/Code
1		25	
2		26	
3		27	
4		28	
5		29	
6		30	
7		31	
8		32	
9		33	
10		34	
11		35	
12		36	
13		37	
14		38	
15		39	
16		40	
17		41	
18		42	
19		43	
20		44	
21		45	
22		46	
23		47	
24		48	

Color Charts
by color

Chart Title	Yellow color chart

	1	2	3	4	5	6	7	8	9	10	11	12	13	14	15
A															
B															
C															
D															
E															
F															
G															
H															
I															
J															
K															
L															
M															
N															
O															

Color Psychology: Yellow

Feelings associated with yellow color:
Curiosity, Caution, Communication, Cheerfulness, Friendliness, Clarity, Cooperation, Happiness, Cowardice, Honor, Hope, Positivity, Humor, Innovation, Uncertainty, Intelligence, Understanding, Warmth, Optimism.

Table Title	Yellow color identifier table A1 - H10

#	Pag.	Pos.	#	Pag.	Pos.	#	Pag.	Pos.	#	Pag.	Pos.	#	Pag.	Pos.
A1			B9			D2			E10			G3		
A2			B10			D3			E11			G4		
A3			B11			D4			E12			G5		
A4			B12			D5			E13			G6		
A5			B13			D6			E14			G7		
A6			B14			D7			E15			G8		
A7			B15			D8			F1			G9		
A8			C1			D9			F2			G10		
A9			C2			D10			F3			G11		
A10			C3			D11			F4			G12		
A11			C4			D12			F5			G13		
A12			C5			D13			F6			G14		
A13			C6			D14			F7			G15		
A14			C7			D15			F8			H1		
A15			C8			E1			F9			H2		
B1			C9			E2			F10			H3		
B2			C10			E3			F11			H4		
B3			C11			E4			F12			H5		
B4			C12			E5			F13			H6		
B5			C13			E6			F14			H7		
B6			C14			E7			F15			H8		
B7			C15			E8			G1			H9		
B8			D1			E9			G2			H10		

Table Title	Yellow color identifier table H11 - O15

#	Pag.	Pos.	#	Pag.	Pos.	#	Pag.	Pos.	#	Pag.	Pos.	#	Pag.	Pos.
H11			J3			K10			M2			N9		
H12			J4			K11			M3			N10		
H13			J5			K12			M4			N11		
H14			J6			K13			M5			N12		
H15			J7			K14			M6			N13		
I1			J8			K15			M7			N14		
I2			J9			L1			M8			N15		
I3			J10			L2			M9			O1		
I4			J11			L3			M10			O2		
I5			J12			L4			M11			O3		
I6			J13			L5			M12			O4		
I7			J14			L6			M13			O5		
I8			J15			L7			M14			O6		
I9			K1			L8			M15			O7		
I10			K2			L9			N1			O8		
I11			K3			L10			N2			O9		
I12			K4			L11			N3			O10		
I13			K5			L12			N4			O11		
I14			K6			L13			N5			O12		
I15			K7			L14			N6			O13		
J1			K8			L15			N7			O14		
J2			K9			M1			N8			O15		

Chart Title	Orange color chart

	1	2	3	4	5	6	7	8	9	10	11	12	13	14	15
A															
B															
C															
D															
E															
F															
G															
H															
I															
J															
K															
L															
M															
N															
O															

Color Psychology: Orange

Feelings associated with orange color:
Action, Enthusiasm, Excitement, Ambition, Fascination, Fun, Artistry, Balance, Innovation, Joviality, Creativity, Vitality, Determination, Warmth, Energy, Youthfulness.

Table Title	Orange color identifier table A1 - H10

#	Pag.	Pos.	#	Pag.	Pos.	#	Pag.	Pos.	#	Pag.	Pos.	#	Pag.	Pos.
A1			B9			D2			E10			G3		
A2			B10			D3			E11			G4		
A3			B11			D4			E12			G5		
A4			B12			D5			E13			G6		
A5			B13			D6			E14			G7		
A6			B14			D7			E15			G8		
A7			B15			D8			F1			G9		
A8			C1			D9			F2			G10		
A9			C2			D10			F3			G11		
A10			C3			D11			F4			G12		
A11			C4			D12			F5			G13		
A12			C5			D13			F6			G14		
A13			C6			D14			F7			G15		
A14			C7			D15			F8			H1		
A15			C8			E1			F9			H2		
B1			C9			E2			F10			H3		
B2			C10			E3			F11			H4		
B3			C11			E4			F12			H5		
B4			C12			E5			F13			H6		
B5			C13			E6			F14			H7		
B6			C14			E7			F15			H8		
B7			C15			E8			G1			H9		
B8			D1			E9			G2			H10		

Table Title	Orange color identifier table H11 - O15

#	Pag.	Pos.	#	Pag.	Pos.	#	Pag.	Pos.	#	Pag.	Pos.	#	Pag.	Pos.
H11			J3			K10			M2			N9		
H12			J4			K11			M3			N10		
H13			J5			K12			M4			N11		
H14			J6			K13			M5			N12		
H15			J7			K14			M6			N13		
I1			J8			K15			M7			N14		
I2			J9			L1			M8			N15		
I3			J10			L2			M9			O1		
I4			J11			L3			M10			O2		
I5			J12			L4			M11			O3		
I6			J13			L5			M12			O4		
I7			J14			L6			M13			O5		
I8			J15			L7			M14			O6		
I9			K1			L8			M15			O7		
I10			K2			L9			N1			O8		
I11			K3			L10			N2			O9		
I12			K4			L11			N3			O10		
I13			K5			L12			N4			O11		
I14			K6			L13			N5			O12		
I15			K7			L14			N6			O13		
J1			K8			L15			N7			O14		
J2			K9			M1			N8			O15		

Chart Title	Red color chart

	1	2	3	4	5	6	7	8	9	10	11	12	13	14	15
A															
B															
C															
D															
E															
F															
G															
H															
I															
J															
K															
L															
M															
N															
O															

Color Psychology: Red

Feelings associated with red color:
Action, Adventure, Force, Heat, Anger, Attention, Courage, Danger, Love, Desire, Passion, Determination, Power, Dynamism, Energy, Romance, Speed, Strength, Strong Emotions, Warmth.

Table Title	Red color identifier table A1 - H10

#	Pag.	Pos.	#	Pag.	Pos.	#	Pag.	Pos.	#	Pag.	Pos.	#	Pag.	Pos.
A1			B9			D2			E10			G3		
A2			B10			D3			E11			G4		
A3			B11			D4			E12			G5		
A4			B12			D5			E13			G6		
A5			B13			D6			E14			G7		
A6			B14			D7			E15			G8		
A7			B15			D8			F1			G9		
A8			C1			D9			F2			G10		
A9			C2			D10			F3			G11		
A10			C3			D11			F4			G12		
A11			C4			D12			F5			G13		
A12			C5			D13			F6			G14		
A13			C6			D14			F7			G15		
A14			C7			D15			F8			H1		
A15			C8			E1			F9			H2		
B1			C9			E2			F10			H3		
B2			C10			E3			F11			H4		
B3			C11			E4			F12			H5		
B4			C12			E5			F13			H6		
B5			C13			E6			F14			H7		
B6			C14			E7			F15			H8		
B7			C15			E8			G1			H9		
B8			D1			E9			G2			H10		

#	Pag.	Pos.	#	Pag.	Pos.	#	Pag.	Pos.	#	Pag.	Pos.	#	Pag.	Pos.
H11			J3			K10			M2			N9		
H12			J4			K11			M3			N10		
H13			J5			K12			M4			N11		
H14			J6			K13			M5			N12		
H15			J7			K14			M6			N13		
I1			J8			K15			M7			N14		
I2			J9			L1			M8			N15		
I3			J10			L2			M9			O1		
I4			J11			L3			M10			O2		
I5			J12			L4			M11			O3		
I6			J13			L5			M12			O4		
I7			J14			L6			M13			O5		
I8			J15			L7			M14			O6		
I9			K1			L8			M15			O7		
I10			K2			L9			N1			O8		
I11			K3			L10			N2			O9		
I12			K4			L11			N3			O10		
I13			K5			L12			N4			O11		
I14			K6			L13			N5			O12		
I15			K7			L14			N6			O13		
J1			K8			L15			N7			O14		
J2			K9			M1			N8			O15		

Table Title: Red color identifier table H11 - O15

Chart Title	Pink color chart

	1	2	3	4	5	6	7	8	9	10	11	12	13	14	15
A															
B															
C															
D															
E															
F															
G															
H															
I															
J															
K															
L															
M															
N															
O															

Color Psychology: Pink

Feelings associated with pink color:
Affection, Appreciation, Goodwill, Beauty, Gratitude, Calmness, Innocence, Delicacy, Emotional Healing, Passivity, Emotional Maturity, Peace, Feminine, Romantic, Flirty, Soft, Floral, Sweet, Friendship, Tranquility, Fun, Truth, Gentleness, Youthfulness.

Table Title	Pink color identifier table A1 - H10

#	Pag.	Pos.	#	Pag.	Pos.	#	Pag.	Pos.	#	Pag.	Pos.	#	Pag.	Pos.
A1			B9			D2			E10			G3		
A2			B10			D3			E11			G4		
A3			B11			D4			E12			G5		
A4			B12			D5			E13			G6		
A5			B13			D6			E14			G7		
A6			B14			D7			E15			G8		
A7			B15			D8			F1			G9		
A8			C1			D9			F2			G10		
A9			C2			D10			F3			G11		
A10			C3			D11			F4			G12		
A11			C4			D12			F5			G13		
A12			C5			D13			F6			G14		
A13			C6			D14			F7			G15		
A14			C7			D15			F8			H1		
A15			C8			E1			F9			H2		
B1			C9			E2			F10			H3		
B2			C10			E3			F11			H4		
B3			C11			E4			F12			H5		
B4			C12			E5			F13			H6		
B5			C13			E6			F14			H7		
B6			C14			E7			F15			H8		
B7			C15			E8			G1			H9		
B8			D1			E9			G2			H10		

Table Title	Pink color identifier table H11 - O15

#	Pag.	Pos.	#	Pag.	Pos.	#	Pag.	Pos.	#	Pag.	Pos.	#	Pag.	Pos.
H11			J3			K10			M2			N9		
H12			J4			K11			M3			N10		
H13			J5			K12			M4			N11		
H14			J6			K13			M5			N12		
H15			J7			K14			M6			N13		
I1			J8			K15			M7			N14		
I2			J9			L1			M8			N15		
I3			J10			L2			M9			O1		
I4			J11			L3			M10			O2		
I5			J12			L4			M11			O3		
I6			J13			L5			M12			O4		
I7			J14			L6			M13			O5		
I8			J15			L7			M14			O6		
I9			K1			L8			M15			O7		
I10			K2			L9			N1			O8		
I11			K3			L10			N2			O9		
I12			K4			L11			N3			O10		
I13			K5			L12			N4			O11		
I14			K6			L13			N5			O12		
I15			K7			L14			N6			O13		
J1			K8			L15			N7			O14		
J2			K9			M1			N8			O15		

Chart Title	Purple color chart

	1	2	3	4	5	6	7	8	9	10	11	12	13	14	15
A															
B															
C															
D															
E															
F															
G															
H															
I															
J															
K															
L															
M															
N															
O															

Color Psychology: Purple

Feelings associated with purple color:
Ambition, Fantasy, Imagination, Celebration, Justice, Luxury, Creativity, Mystery, Deeper Truth, Nobility, Dignity, Education, Royalty, Elegance, Sensuality, Empathy, Sophistication, Enlightenment, Spirituality, Success, Wealth, Fame, Wisdom.

Table Title: Purple color identifier table A1 - H10

#	Pag.	Pos.	#	Pag.	Pos.	#	Pag.	Pos.	#	Pag.	Pos.	#	Pag.	Pos.
A1			B9			D2			E10			G3		
A2			B10			D3			E11			G4		
A3			B11			D4			E12			G5		
A4			B12			D5			E13			G6		
A5			B13			D6			E14			G7		
A6			B14			D7			E15			G8		
A7			B15			D8			F1			G9		
A8			C1			D9			F2			G10		
A9			C2			D10			F3			G11		
A10			C3			D11			F4			G12		
A11			C4			D12			F5			G13		
A12			C5			D13			F6			G14		
A13			C6			D14			F7			G15		
A14			C7			D15			F8			H1		
A15			C8			E1			F9			H2		
B1			C9			E2			F10			H3		
B2			C10			E3			F11			H4		
B3			C11			E4			F12			H5		
B4			C12			E5			F13			H6		
B5			C13			E6			F14			H7		
B6			C14			E7			F15			H8		
B7			C15			E8			G1			H9		
B8			D1			E9			G2			H10		

#	Pag.	Pos.	#	Pag.	Pos.	#	Pag.	Pos.	#	Pag.	Pos.	#	Pag.	Pos.
H11			J3			K10			M2			N9		
H12			J4			K11			M3			N10		
H13			J5			K12			M4			N11		
H14			J6			K13			M5			N12		
H15			J7			K14			M6			N13		
I1			J8			K15			M7			N14		
I2			J9			L1			M8			N15		
I3			J10			L2			M9			O1		
I4			J11			L3			M10			O2		
I5			J12			L4			M11			O3		
I6			J13			L5			M12			O4		
I7			J14			L6			M13			O5		
I8			J15			L7			M14			O6		
I9			K1			L8			M15			O7		
I10			K2			L9			N1			O8		
I11			K3			L10			N2			O9		
I12			K4			L11			N3			O10		
I13			K5			L12			N4			O11		
I14			K6			L13			N5			O12		
I15			K7			L14			N6			O13		
J1			K8			L15			N7			O14		
J2			K9			M1			N8			O15		

Chart Title	Blue color chart

	1	2	3	4	5	6	7	8	9	10	11	12	13	14	15
A															
B															
C															
D															
E															
F															
G															
H															
I															
J															
K															
L															
M															
N															
O															

Color Psychology: Blue

Feelings associated with blue color:
Confidence, Calm, Contemplation, Cleanliness, Devotion, Comfort, Dignity, Communication, Establishment, Faith, Professionalism, Gentleness, Protection, Security, Inner Strength, Serenity, Inspiration, Integrity, Sincerity, Intelligence, Success, Loyalty, Order, Trust, Peace, Understanding, Power, Unity.

Table Title	Blue color identifier table A1 - H10

#	Pag.	Pos.	#	Pag.	Pos.	#	Pag.	Pos.	#	Pag.	Pos.	#	Pag.	Pos.
A1			B9			D2			E10			G3		
A2			B10			D3			E11			G4		
A3			B11			D4			E12			G5		
A4			B12			D5			E13			G6		
A5			B13			D6			E14			G7		
A6			B14			D7			E15			G8		
A7			B15			D8			F1			G9		
A8			C1			D9			F2			G10		
A9			C2			D10			F3			G11		
A10			C3			D11			F4			G12		
A11			C4			D12			F5			G13		
A12			C5			D13			F6			G14		
A13			C6			D14			F7			G15		
A14			C7			D15			F8			H1		
A15			C8			E1			F9			H2		
B1			C9			E2			F10			H3		
B2			C10			E3			F11			H4		
B3			C11			E4			F12			H5		
B4			C12			E5			F13			H6		
B5			C13			E6			F14			H7		
B6			C14			E7			F15			H8		
B7			C15			E8			G1			H9		
B8			D1			E9			G2			H10		

Table Title	Blue color identifier table H11 - O15

#	Pag.	Pos.	#	Pag.	Pos.	#	Pag.	Pos.	#	Pag.	Pos.	#	Pag.	Pos.
H11			J3			K10			M2			N9		
H12			J4			K11			M3			N10		
H13			J5			K12			M4			N11		
H14			J6			K13			M5			N12		
H15			J7			K14			M6			N13		
I1			J8			K15			M7			N14		
I2			J9			L1			M8			N15		
I3			J10			L2			M9			O1		
I4			J11			L3			M10			O2		
I5			J12			L4			M11			O3		
I6			J13			L5			M12			O4		
I7			J14			L6			M13			O5		
I8			J15			L7			M14			O6		
I9			K1			L8			M15			O7		
I10			K2			L9			N1			O8		
I11			K3			L10			N2			O9		
I12			K4			L11			N3			O10		
I13			K5			L12			N4			O11		
I14			K6			L13			N5			O12		
I15			K7			L14			N6			O13		
J1			K8			L15			N7			O14		
J2			K9			M1			N8			O15		

Chart Title	Turquoise and Teal colors chart

	1	2	3	4	5	6	7	8	9	10	11	12	13	14	15
A															
B															
C															
D															
E															
F															
G															
H															
I															
J															
K															
L															
M															
N															
O															

Color Psychology: Turquoise and Teal

Feelings associated with turquoise and teal colors:
Serenity, Balance, Introspection, Emotional Control, Creativity, Calmness, Refreshing, Clarity, Elegance, Tranquility, Dignity, Emotional Healing, Trust, Devotion, Protection,.

Table Title	Turquoise and Teal colors identifier table A1 - H10

#	Pag.	Pos.	#	Pag.	Pos.	#	Pag.	Pos.	#	Pag.	Pos.	#	Pag.	Pos.
A1			B9			D2			E10			G3		
A2			B10			D3			E11			G4		
A3			B11			D4			E12			G5		
A4			B12			D5			E13			G6		
A5			B13			D6			E14			G7		
A6			B14			D7			E15			G8		
A7			B15			D8			F1			G9		
A8			C1			D9			F2			G10		
A9			C2			D10			F3			G11		
A10			C3			D11			F4			G12		
A11			C4			D12			F5			G13		
A12			C5			D13			F6			G14		
A13			C6			D14			F7			G15		
A14			C7			D15			F8			H1		
A15			C8			E1			F9			H2		
B1			C9			E2			F10			H3		
B2			C10			E3			F11			H4		
B3			C11			E4			F12			H5		
B4			C12			E5			F13			H6		
B5			C13			E6			F14			H7		
B6			C14			E7			F15			H8		
B7			C15			E8			G1			H9		
B8			D1			E9			G2			H10		

Table Title	Turquoise and Teal colors identifier table H11 - O15																

#	Pag.	Pos.	#	Pag.	Pos.	#	Pag.	Pos.	#	Pag.	Pos.	#	Pag.	Pos.	#	Pag.	Pos.
H11			J3			K10			M2			N9						
H12			J4			K11			M3			N10						
H13			J5			K12			M4			N11						
H14			J6			K13			M5			N12						
H15			J7			K14			M6			N13						
I1			J8			K15			M7			N14						
I2			J9			L1			M8			N15						
I3			J10			L2			M9			O1						
I4			J11			L3			M10			O2						
I5			J12			L4			M11			O3						
I6			J13			L5			M12			O4						
I7			J14			L6			M13			O5						
I8			J15			L7			M14			O6						
I9			K1			L8			M15			O7						
I10			K2			L9			N1			O8						
I11			K3			L10			N2			O9						
I12			K4			L11			N3			O10						
I13			K5			L12			N4			O11						
I14			K6			L13			N5			O12						
I15			K7			L14			N6			O13						
J1			K8			L15			N7			O14						
J2			K9			M1			N8			O15						

Chart Title	Green color chart

	1	2	3	4	5	6	7	8	9	10	11	12	13	14	15
A															
B															
C															
D															
E															
F															
G															
H															
I															
J															
K															
L															
M															
N															
O															

Color Psychology: Green

Feelings associated with green color:
Abundance, Health, Hope, Endurance, Immortality, Environmental, Fertility, Natural, Freshness, Good Luck, Plentiful, Growth, Renewal, Harmony, Stability, Healing, Tranquility.

Table Title	Green color identifier table A1 - H10

#	Pag.	Pos.	#	Pag.	Pos.	#	Pag.	Pos.	#	Pag.	Pos.	#	Pag.	Pos.
A1			B9			D2			E10			G3		
A2			B10			D3			E11			G4		
A3			B11			D4			E12			G5		
A4			B12			D5			E13			G6		
A5			B13			D6			E14			G7		
A6			B14			D7			E15			G8		
A7			B15			D8			F1			G9		
A8			C1			D9			F2			G10		
A9			C2			D10			F3			G11		
A10			C3			D11			F4			G12		
A11			C4			D12			F5			G13		
A12			C5			D13			F6			G14		
A13			C6			D14			F7			G15		
A14			C7			D15			F8			H1		
A15			C8			E1			F9			H2		
B1			C9			E2			F10			H3		
B2			C10			E3			F11			H4		
B3			C11			E4			F12			H5		
B4			C12			E5			F13			H6		
B5			C13			E6			F14			H7		
B6			C14			E7			F15			H8		
B7			C15			E8			G1			H9		
B8			D1			E9			G2			H10		

#	Pag.	Pos.	#	Pag.	Pos.	#	Pag.	Pos.	#	Pag.	Pos.	#	Pag.	Pos.
H11			J3			K10			M2			N9		
H12			J4			K11			M3			N10		
H13			J5			K12			M4			N11		
H14			J6			K13			M5			N12		
H15			J7			K14			M6			N13		
I1			J8			K15			M7			N14		
I2			J9			L1			M8			N15		
I3			J10			L2			M9			O1		
I4			J11			L3			M10			O2		
I5			J12			L4			M11			O3		
I6			J13			L5			M12			O4		
I7			J14			L6			M13			O5		
I8			J15			L7			M14			O6		
I9			K1			L8			M15			O7		
I10			K2			L9			N1			O8		
I11			K3			L10			N2			O9		
I12			K4			L11			N3			O10		
I13			K5			L12			N4			O11		
I14			K6			L13			N5			O12		
I15			K7			L14			N6			O13		
J1			K8			L15			N7			O14		
J2			K9			M1			N8			O15		

Chart Title	Brown, Gray and Black colors chart

	1	2	3	4	5	6	7	8	9	10	11	12	13	14	15
A															
B															
C															
D															
E															
F															
G															
H															
I															
J															
K															
L															
M															
N															
O															

Color Psychology: Brown, Gray and Black

Brown: *Calmness, Comfort, Credibility, Natural, Passivity, Endurance, Practicality, Fertility, Productivity, Friendship, Reliability, Roughness, Intimacy, Sensuality, Stability, Serious, Strength, Simplicity, Solid, Utility.*

Gray: *Practicality, Professionalism, Quality, Dignity, Dullness, Reliability, Durability, Respect, Intelligence, Security, Maturity, Solid, Modesty, Sophistication, Stability.*

Black: *Power, Prestige, Protection, Boldness, Secrecy, Classic, Seriousness, Conservative, Sophistication, Distinctive, Strength, Elegance, Style, Formality, High Quality, Wealth, Mystery.*

Table Title	Brown, Gray, Black colors identifier table A1 - H10

#	Pag.	Pos.	#	Pag.	Pos.	#	Pag.	Pos.	#	Pag.	Pos.	#	Pag.	Pos.
A1			B9			D2			E10			G3		
A2			B10			D3			E11			G4		
A3			B11			D4			E12			G5		
A4			B12			D5			E13			G6		
A5			B13			D6			E14			G7		
A6			B14			D7			E15			G8		
A7			B15			D8			F1			G9		
A8			C1			D9			F2			G10		
A9			C2			D10			F3			G11		
A10			C3			D11			F4			G12		
A11			C4			D12			F5			G13		
A12			C5			D13			F6			G14		
A13			C6			D14			F7			G15		
A14			C7			D15			F8			H1		
A15			C8			E1			F9			H2		
B1			C9			E2			F10			H3		
B2			C10			E3			F11			H4		
B3			C11			E4			F12			H5		
B4			C12			E5			F13			H6		
B5			C13			E6			F14			H7		
B6			C14			E7			F15			H8		
B7			C15			E8			G1			H9		
B8			D1			E9			G2			H10		

Table Title	Brown, Gray, Black colors identifier table H11 - O15

#	Pag.	Pos.	#	Pag.	Pos.	#	Pag.	Pos.	#	Pag.	Pos.	#	Pag.	Pos.
H11			J3			K10			M2			N9		
H12			J4			K11			M3			N10		
H13			J5			K12			M4			N11		
H14			J6			K13			M5			N12		
H15			J7			K14			M6			N13		
I1			J8			K15			M7			N14		
I2			J9			L1			M8			N15		
I3			J10			L2			M9			O1		
I4			J11			L3			M10			O2		
I5			J12			L4			M11			O3		
I6			J13			L5			M12			O4		
I7			J14			L6			M13			O5		
I8			J15			L7			M14			O6		
I9			K1			L8			M15			O7		
I10			K2			L9			N1			O8		
I11			K3			L10			N2			O9		
I12			K4			L11			N3			O10		
I13			K5			L12			N4			O11		
I14			K6			L13			N5			O12		
I15			K7			L14			N6			O13		
J1			K8			L15			N7			O14		
J2			K9			M1			N8			O15		

Blending Charts

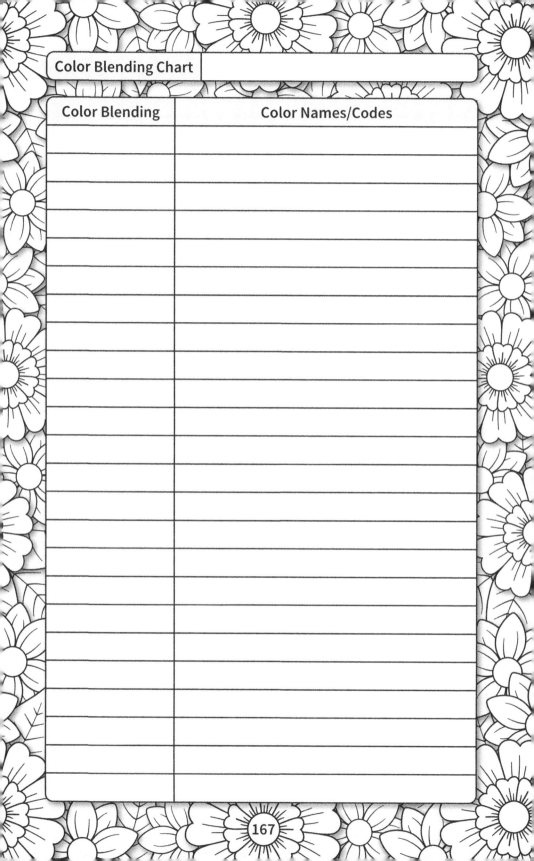

Color Blending Chart

Color Blending	Color Names/Codes

Color Blending Chart

Color Blending	Color Names/Codes

Color Blending Chart

Color Blending	Color Names/Codes

Color Blending Chart

Color Blending	Color Names/Codes

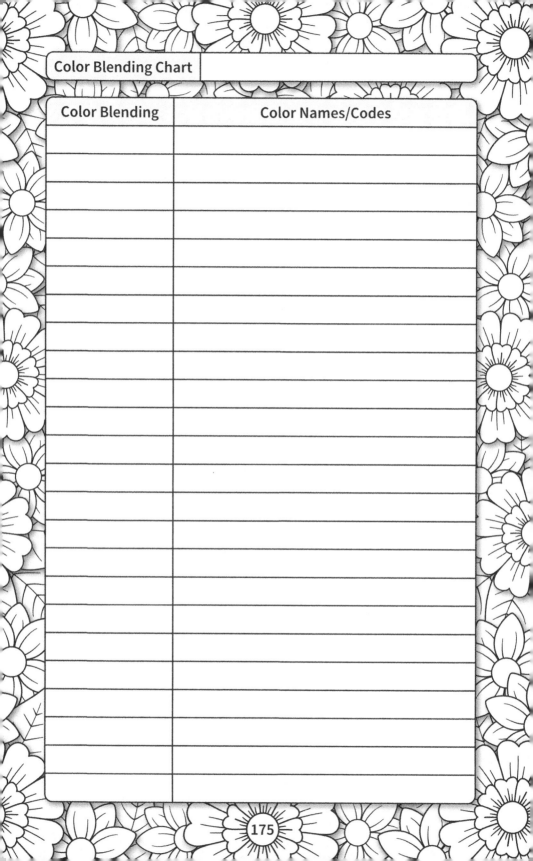

Color Blending Chart

Color Blending	Color Names/Codes

Color
Palettes

Color Palettes Chart

Color	Color Name/Code	Color	Color Name/Code

Color Palettes Chart

Color	Color Name/Code	Color	Color Name/Code

Color Palettes Chart

Color	Color Name/Code	Color	Color Name/Code

Color Palettes Chart

Color	Color Name/Code	Color	Color Name/Code

Color Palettes Chart

Color	Color Name/Code	Color	Color Name/Code

Color Palettes Chart

Color	Color Name/Code	Color	Color Name/Code

Notes

Notes

Notes

Notes

Notes

Notes

Made in the USA
Monee, IL
04 January 2023

24488992R00111